CW00550394

EDWARDIAN HOUSE

ORIGINAL FEATURES AND FITTINGS

Trevor Yorke

COUNTRYSIDE BOOKS
NEWBURY BERKSHIRE

First published 2013
© Trevor Yorke 2013

All rights reserved. No reproduction permitted
without the prior permission of the publisher:

COUNTRYSIDE BOOKS
3 Catherine Road
Newbury, Berkshire

To view our complete range of books, please
visit us at www.countrysidebooks.co.uk

ISBN 978-1-84674-312-2

Photographs and illustrations by the author.

Designed by Peter Davies, Nautilus Design
Produced by The Letterworks Ltd., Reading
Printed by Berforts Information Press, Oxford

CONTENTS

Introduction

Houses built between the last decade of the 19th century and the outbreak of war in 1914, have distinctive characteristics which make them stand out from the crowd. The Edwardian suburbs were rapidly expanding, filled with newly-built terraces, semis and detached houses. These homes were inspired by building styles from Britain's historic past, with Arts and Crafts or Art Nouveau details, and built along wide, paved streets that were interspersed by patches of greenery. The houses were also of a quality rarely matched before or since, built with bricks, timber and metalwork that could last for centuries.

This quality has not always been appreciated in the past. Many properties have had doors, windows, or interior features replaced in an attempt to make them more fashionable or draught free. In some streets, there have been so many changes made that it can be hard to visualise how the houses originally appeared. Today though, there is a greater appreciation of buildings from this Edwardian period. Houses renovated or restored to something like their original form have generally created greater financial and emotional value.

This book introduces the reader to the styles and forms of the original features and fittings, which builders in this period would have used. It uses my own colour drawings, diagrams and photographs to help explain how features like the windows, doors and porches on the outside and the fireplaces, stairs and bathrooms inside would have appeared when their tenants (most people rented their home before the First World War) first moved into these new homes.

Each chapter includes notes on the variety of styles, why they were made and finished in such a way, and the characteristic details to look out for from this period. There are tips on how to maintain and improve the original fittings in your own house, if you are fortunate enough to still have them. If they have been removed, there is a list of websites at the end of the book which can help you find the appropriate parts.

For anyone who simply wants to recognise the styles, understand how Edwardian houses originally appeared, and appreciate their Arts and Crafts and Art Nouveau details, this book makes a colourful and easy to follow introduction to the subject.

Trevor Yorke

For more information visit:
www.trevoryorke.co.uk
and follow me on facebook at:
trevoryorke-author

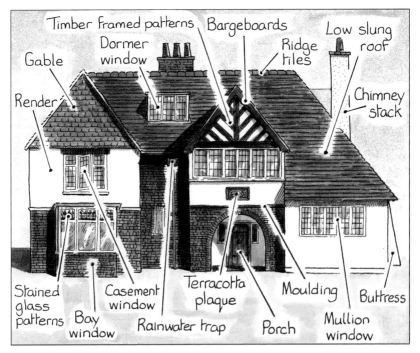

An Edwardian exterior and interior with labels of key parts

The Edwardian House

Edward VII had been Prince of Wales for fifty-nine years when he ascended the throne upon the death of his mother, Queen Victoria, in 1901. Yet, in his short nine year reign, this social and affable monarch lightened the image of the Royal family, introduced pomp and ceremony, and healed rifts with European countries, especially France. The period named after him may have been brief, but its influence of events and distinctive fashions have spread over a wider timescale. We apply the term Edwardian to the forms and styles of houses which first emerged in the 1890s, and were still being built in the early 1920s.

At the top end of the market, were architect-designed homes in a wide variety of styles. Their forms varied from the tall and stout mansions that dominated their surroundings, to low profile houses which complemented the landscape. The façade of the building could be finished in patterned brickwork, contrasting masonry, timber framing and pebbledash or roughcast, while Arts and Crafts designers emphasised the use of local materials. Balconies were a distinctive feature of this more colourful period, while new kitchens and service wings gave servants who were used to working below ground, much improved conditions. Although the styles were clearly inspired by the past, the form of the buildings could be inventive and new, no more so than in some of the interiors designed by leading architects.

FIG 0.1: WAVERTREE GARDEN SUBURB, LIVERPOOL: *In this period the first serious attempts were made at building spacious housing set amongst trees and green spaces, with rents low enough for the working classes. Some were factory estates, others new suburbs designed by leading architects and funded by wealthy philanthropists. Houses were usually in a Neo Georgian or Arts and Crafts style, as here at Wavertree, Liverpool, and helped inspire post war council housing.*

They divided up large spaces by varying heights, inserting galleries and controlling light. In some of the most daring houses, a puritanical simplicity and plain natural surfaces gave a hint of 20th century Modernism. Although the inside of most houses was still cluttered, with grand decorative pieces and busy patterns, the overall effect was lighter and more airy than that of a generation or two before, with items grouped rather than just scattered around.

Below this top strata lay the mass of suburban housing, built to cater for the needs and aspirations of a booming middle class. Some were sizable detached houses, designed by a local architect or notable builder in the latest styles. Most, however, were semis or terraces erected by speculative builders (those who built and then found buyers or tenants), with layouts and façades that were considered stylistically safe and appealed to a wide audience. The form and layout of the house had to be practical and conventional so as not to put off potential tenants, but with a few cosmetic details added to the exterior to reflect a fashionable style. Railways, trams and the London underground made cheaper agricultural land that was further away from city centres accessible to commuters. This meant that builders were able to use the money saved on buying the plot, to make houses wider and lavish them with additional features like large hallways, bay windows and gardens. White painted porches, chimneys set halfway down the slope of the roof and small balconies are all distinctive of this period.

The styles of houses which the leading architects created and the speculative builders copied, were inspired by our historic past and a resurgence of interest in Classical architecture. These houses were deemed more appropriate for the grander state buildings being erected at the time, as opposed to the more humble domestic styles. This Edwardian Baroque style shaped some country houses. A more domestic Classical style, based upon buildings from the late 17th and early 18th century and called the Neo Georgian, was widely used (although

FIG 0.2: *An Arts and Crafts house (top) and a Neo Georgian house (below).*

FIG 0.3. BLACKWELL, ARTS AND CRAFTS HOUSE, WINDERMERE: *Although the exterior might be in one specific historic style, it was common practice to use different sources of inspiration for each of the principal rooms inside. Many were inspired by 17th and 18th century English styles, featuring fittings and furniture with heavier ornamentation and busier designs than the originals. Elizabethan or Jacobean style was often used in dining rooms, lighter Queen Anne or Chippendale furnishings in the drawing room, Oriental or Moorish decoration in the billiard room and more frivolous Louis XV in the boudoir. Arts and Crafts interiors could be equally varied, but were simpler and more inventive in form. They aimed to emphasise the natural texture of the material, as in the hall at Blackwell, Windermere, pictured above. In many examples, however, the style is not clear as it has been misinterpreted from the original and become rather lost in the mass of eclectic decoration, plants and ornaments.*

the houses which inspired it came before George I ascended the throne). It had symmetrical façades, dormer windows in steep pitched roofs and sash windows divided up by numerous glazing bars. Arts and Crafts houses could appear more humble, with low slung roofs, long elongated window openings, deep recessed porches and vernacular materials exposed across the façade. This rather exclusive style was watered down for the mass market, with more conventionally laid out houses featuring leaded casement windows, vertically planked doors, and splashes of pebbledash, hanging tiles and timber framing, in what were usually termed Tudoresque or Mock Tudor homes. The Queen Anne style, with its rich red brickwork, white painted woodwork and Dutch gables had evolved in the 1880s and was still popular on terraces in the following decades. Despite a closer relationship with France and the continent, Art Nouveau, with its strangely curved natural forms, was too daring and foreign for most tastes. It was, however, more accepted for metal, ceramic and coloured glass decorative pieces, both inside and outside the house. It is also important to remember that a large number of houses will be found with features taken from a number of these styles, creating eclectic façades which could best be labeled, Edwardian!

FIG 0.4: *Examples of Edwardian style suburban housing with wider frontages than their Victorian counterparts, ample use of hanging tiles, timber framing and pebbledash and decorative timber work around the front door.*

CHAPTER I

Windows
Sashes, Casements, Coloured Glass

FIG 1.1: *Part of the character of Edwardian houses is their bold, three dimensional façades full of texture and colour. The key fittings in these compositions are the windows. A wide selection of shapes, patterns and form were distinctive of this period.*

The Edwardian period is renowned for its variety of styles and quality of buildings, and this is evident in the windows which were fitted. There were vertically sliding sash windows, side hinged casement windows, bay windows in all shapes and sizes and long horizontal mullion windows. In addition to these

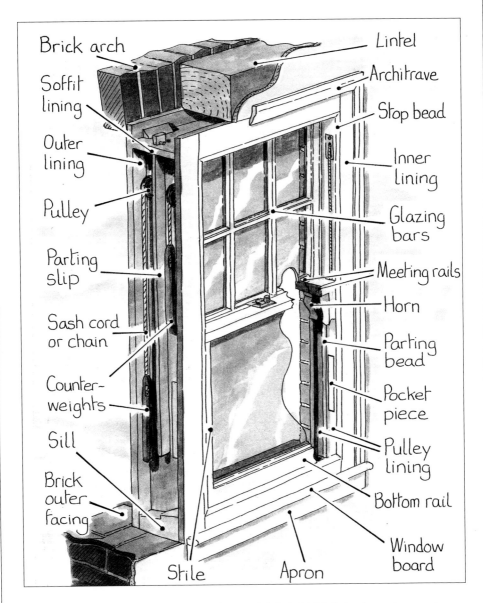

FIG 1.2: *The inside face of a sash window with labels highlighting its various parts. Note the cut away on the right shows the junction between the meeting rails, which were bevelled so that the lower would press firmly against the upper one, to cut out draughts. It has a step to prevent the fastener being slipped open by a knife.*

were numerous types of small projecting window, dormers set in the slope of the roof, and openings filled with colourful leaded lights.

Sash Windows

A sash is a frame with glazing. A sash window is made by inserting two of these frames into an outer frame, so at least one can be opened vertically or sideways. Edwardian types were double hung, in that both the upper and lower sash could be moved up and down. This process was made easier by having metal counterweights hidden in the outer frame, or sash box, and linked to the sashes by cords or chains. Examples from the 1890s and early 1900s are distinctive in often having the upper sash divided up by glazing bars, to suit the popular

FIG 1.3: *Examples of sash windows from the 1890s and early 1900s. The most common arrangement on middle class houses was to have the upper sash divided by glazing bars and the lower left clear (top left pair), although there were also variations of this with additional pieces creating novel patterns (bottom right pair). Neo Georgian style houses had both divided up (top right pair), often with the horns still fitted, unlike the originals they replicated. Windows were also set in pairs, or had thinner flanking windows each side (bottom left pair). Note that the sash box could now be fitted flush, or even protrude, from the face of the wall.*

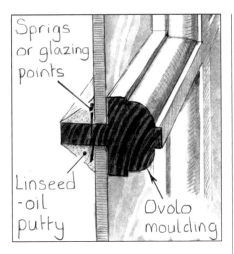

FIG 1.4: *A section through a sash window glazing bar detail. A simple quadrant within a right angle, called an ovolo moulding, was the usual profile found on sash windows from this period. The glass is fitted from the outside and held in place by small nails called sprigs, or triangular metal glazing points (as found on the back of picture frames), with these covered up by a chamfered line of linseed oil putty.*

FIG 1.5: HORNS: *The meeting rails were traditionally joined to the stiles by a simple dovetail joint. This was not a problem as there were numerous glazing*

Renovating Windows

Sash windows were designed to be repairable and with the excellent quality of wood which was generally used, they should last for centuries. The stop bead can be prized away so the lower sash can be lifted out and cords disconnected, and then the parting bead removed to do the same for the upper one. With the sashes removed maintenance is straightforward. The cords or chains can be replaced, frames sanded down to make them run smoothly, rotten wood treated or renewed, joints repaired and replacement glass fitted. These are all DIY jobs, or tasks a local builder can do for you. However, there are now numerous nationwide companies who will not only renovate sash windows, but also fit brush seals around the gaps to ensure all drafts are blocked. Further energy efficiency improvements can be made by fitting modern discrete secondary glazing. This creates a large gap between the glazing and the original window, and therefore reduces more noise from outside than would be the case with uPVC double glazed windows alone (the same applies to casement windows).

bars to keep the sashes rigid. But when they were no longer fitted in the Victorian period, it became necessary to strengthen the joint. The stile on the upper sash was extended down so a stronger mortise and tenon joint could be fitted, and the protruding part beneath called the horn (left) had a chamfered or curving profile. These horns are found on most Edwardian sash windows, even where glazing bars were fitted.

FIG 1.6: BLIND BOXES: *Exterior blinds, which were hidden behind a box at the top of the windows, were fitted on the south facing front of some high class houses. While the blinds have usually gone, a plain timber box, as in this example, or a scalloped recess have sometimes survived.*

17th and 18th century revival styles, while the lower one was left clear for an unobstructed view. The 1894 London Building Act relaxed the rules designed to reduce fire risk, so that the outer sash box no longer had to be recessed behind four inches of brick or masonry (as shown in Fig 1.2). Windows became flush with the face of the wall, or projected out from it.

Casement Windows

These wooden or metal framed windows had tall, thin frames set vertically in a row. Some of the frames would be hinged at the side, so they could be opened for ventilation. Although this style became

FIG 1.7: PULLEYS: *These are metal wheels on a spindle over which the sash cords ran. They were usually encased in a small metal chamber set within the sash box. Better quality versions had a brass piece over the front (as in this example) and a brass wheel, some also ran on ball bearings for a smoother action. An alternative were tape balances, which were like a modern spring loaded tape measure, and didn't require counterweights.*

FIG 1.8: SASH FASTENERS: *These are a pair of metal plates on top of the meeting rails, with a small bar which slides between the two sides to lock them in place. They could be purchased to match other ironmongery in the room and some had catches or patent designs to prevent them being opened from outside. Handles, hooks or slots were also fitted to the base of sashes to make lifting them easier. Usually in brass, but black iron (referred to as Japanned) was also used.*

FIG 1.9: *Examples of casement windows from the 1890s and early 1900s. Most had wooden frames at this date, but metal ones were available, although they did not become widespread until after the First World War. The most common form was to have the short upper section filled with coloured glass, leaded lights or divided up by glazing bars (top row), and the taller lower part to be clear. Elongated versions filled with glazing bars or leaded lights (bottom row) were fitted in Arts and Crafts, Tudoresque and some Neo Georgian houses. The glass was usually set in rectangles, whereas the original pieces on which they were based were diamond shaped, (although these were also copied).*

standard during the 20th century, it was only beginning to challenge the dominant sash window in the Edwardian period. Casement windows, fitted in the early 1900s, had a row of small top lights, which usually featured coloured glass patterns (see Fig 1.13), while Tudoresque style houses had rectangular leaded lights with clear glass. It was also distinctive of this period to have wooden casement windows projecting from the front of the house, sometimes by just a matter of inches, in other cases forming a more prominent oriel or bay window.

Mullion windows

These elongated low windows, divided up into numerous tall, thin lights by mullions (vertical divisions fixed within the frame), were a distinctive feature of

Arts and Crafts inspired houses. The 16th and 17th century windows upon which they were based had the mullion set at 45 degrees in a diamond-shaped socket in the sill, but Edwardian replicas were often set square, with only a simple moulding down the side, or none at all. They were made of stone, timber or brick, the latter usually splayed (angled) with iron frames set within each light, some of which were hinged so they could be opened. Mullion

FIG 1.10: CASEMENT STAYS AND FASTENERS: *Iron stays along the bottom of the window with holes to allow the frame to be held open in a variety of positions, and metal fasteners up the side to lock it into position, were available in styles and materials similar to other ironmongery in the house. However, as casements tended to be fitted on more cottage style houses, black iron stays and fasteners inspired by Arts and Crafts designs were also popular.*

FIG 1.11 (RIGHT): *Examples of stone, brick and timber mullion windows from the 1890s and early 1900s. The openings were usually squared off (top,) or had a simple chamfer (lower three). Each light was filled with rectangular quarries (individual panes of glass) set in cames (the soft metal strips which held them).*

FIG 1.13: BAY WINDOWS: *These were the height of fashion in the Edwardian period, as their ability to let in more light and create a bright seating area was appreciated. They could be found on most houses, ranging from large two storey structures with a gable above, down to simple protrusions on the ground floor below a continuous porch which ran across the façade. Renovation of bay windows is not only important to retain the historic appeal of a property, but also because the vertical members carry the load from above. Problems often arise with modern uPVC replacements, which may not be strong enough or correctly fitted. Secondary glazing inside may be a better solution to reduce noise and improve energy efficiency.*

FIG 1.12 (ABOVE): *The relaxing of the rules concerning the fire risk of timber across the facade, meant that architects could now be more adventurous in their window design. Small triangular shaped projecting windows, ones which cut through a corner, a variety of dormers, and oval openings as pictured here, are distinctive of this period. Shallow brick arches above windows (bottom) and dormers with the roof raised over it in a curve like an eyebrow were also fitted.*

windows were often found on high class houses, there might also be some fine ironwork on the stays and catches.

Glass patterns

Stained or coloured glass patterns and the skills to make them had been revived from the 1840s and had become a distinctive feature of the finest Gothic styled Victorian houses. By the end of the 19th century, these patterns were being mass produced. Decorative glass was used in the glazed sections of front doors and the top lights of casement

FIG 1.14: *Colourful glass patterns are distinctive of windows from the 1890s and early 1900s, as in these examples. They could be formed from geometric glazing bars or feature heraldic motifs (top row), use flowing floral patterns (centre row) or have more rigid geometric designs (bottom row). They were usually based upon a rectangular framework, and often used glass with a patterned or textured surface.*

windows, sometimes even filling the whole opening. Stylised floral designs were the most widely found, with flowing stems and simple flower and leaf shapes. Heraldic symbols, like shields and banners, were popular on Tudoresque houses, while detailed painted elements recreating Medieval stained glass could be found on Arts and Crafts inspired houses. The most up-to-date housing featured heavily stylised floral patterns, inspired by Art Nouveau designers, like Charles Rennie Mackintosh.

FIG 1.15: OLD GLASS: *By the turn of the 20th century methods of glass production had improved. It had become relatively inexpensive and available in a wide range of colours and textures, however, clear panes still had an undulating surface which distorted reflections (top). Modern float glass (bottom), with its perfect smooth finish, can seem inappropriate in a house which is over a hundred years old. If your house is within a conservation area or is a listed building, you might have to retain the original glass.*

FIG 1.16: WINDOW FRAME COLOURS: *Throughout the Edwardian home, it was common for any exposed softwood to be painted and grained to appear like a quality hardwood. This was true for the exterior surface of many window frames especially in terraced housing. However, white painted frames were becoming more popular, especially on Queen Anne and Neo Georgian style houses. Although this was a more subdued tone than the brilliant whites used today. Some windows were also painted with a dark colour around the outside of the frame and a white or cream on the inner edges, although this is an arrangement which was much more common after the First World War.*

 *Doors*

Handles, Knobs, Letter Boxes, Glass

FIG 2.1: *The front door was the focal point of a façade and reflected the style of the house, as in this Neo Georgian example. It also gave the owner an opportunity to display their status and taste with apparently high quality materials and ornately decorated surfaces. The Edwardians more than anyone else took these ideas to heart, and created the most dazzling and colourful doors.*

The variety of styles of Edwardian houses resulted in a wide choice of front doors to complement them. The four panelled door (two tall panels above two shorter ones), which had been universally popular for much of the Victorian period, was still used. However, by the 1890s this style had been joined by ones which combined vertical, horizontal or full width panels to create unique designs. Doors were also made inspired by Arts and Crafts houses; they were composed of vertical planks with protruding strips covering the joints and perhaps a small window near the top. Another distinctive style which first appeared at the end of the 19th century, and became universal after the First World War, were those which seemed to reverse the traditional tall panels above short. Instead, they featured a glazed upper third with usually three vertical panels below.

Although some of the door styles can

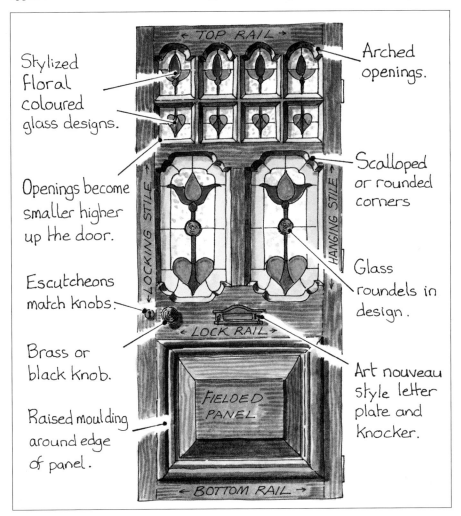

FIG 2.2: *An Edwardian door with labels of key parts and distinctive features.*

FIG 2.3: *Examples of doors from houses built in the 1890s and early 1900s. Variants with a glazed upper third and panelled lower section (1st four from the top left) were coming into vogue, while the traditional four panelled door had given way to more playful arrangements with deep moulding to emphasise the panels (top right and bottom left). The most distinctive type of the period were those with square and arched glazed openings stacked upon each other (centre bottom). There was always scope for more unusual designs, as in the example on the bottom right.*

be found in earlier and later periods, there are characteristics which are distinctly Edwardian. Glazed openings in the upper sections were very common, usually featuring coloured glass patterns. Halls were often still narrow and dark at this date. Therefore, the designs needed to let in as much light as possible, yet

FIG 2.4: *Arts and Crafts and Tudoresque style houses usually had doors based upon traditional plank and batten types (vertical planks held together by a series of horizontal battens on the inside) as pictured here. Vertical strips covered the joints and they often had an arched top, or were set in a deep arched recess. Their plain surfaces made an ideal background for elaborate cast iron door furniture like drop ring handles and decorative strap hinges. This type was not usually fitted to terraces, where the dark narrow hall required light to come through a glazed section of the door.*

at the same time to retain the privacy of residents through the use of textured and coloured glass. The panels on the door could be made to appear deeper by adding a raised moulding around their outer edge, rather than by using thicker timber, and they were usually fielded (raised centre section with chamfered edges). It was also common for corners of panels to be rounded, usually just at the top, and for full and half width panels to be combined in the same door. A feature which is almost unique to the 1890s and early 1900s, is the use of rows of increasingly smaller openings stacked upon each other (see Fig 2.2).

Door Glass

The use of coloured and patterned glass within the front door made a statement of the owner's status and taste to those approaching the house. While in the day it filled the hall with splashes of colour and sparkling light, at night it cast a warm and welcoming glow. As with the pieces fitted in windows (see Fig 1.14), the finest examples were made by craftsmen, who had a wide range of patterned and coloured glass by which to make their unique designs. On most middle class houses, the glass was bought as a ready-made sheet from stained glass studios or builders merchants. In the 1890s, rather

FIG 2.5: *Examples of leaded glass patterns from late 19th and early 20th century glazed doors. Designs are dominated by florals, some stylised with a vertical central stem, others with sinuous stems and more naturalistic flowers. Geometric patterns, with a central painted or coloured glass feature, were also popular. In general, Edwardian glazed doors were busier and more colourful than 1930s types.*

old fashioned spiky Gothic designs, containing brown and amber pieces with painted scenes in the centre, could still be found. But by the early 1900s, Arts and Crafts and Art Nouveau inspired patterns with simpler, stylised floral designs and more cheerful colours were dominant.

A single opening filled with these colourful patterns is called a leaded light. It consists of lead strips called *cames* with an 'H' shaped profile, which are soldered together around the piece of glass. To strengthen large sheets, thin metal saddle bars could be inserted across the inside and connected to the lead by pieces of copper wire. There was a wide range of glass types available to the glazier from which to form his design.

FIG 2.6: *A detail from a double door, with birds painted in the central section and stylised flowers below. Note the period door furniture and white glazed house number. The scalloped decorative wood around the letter box is called an* apron.

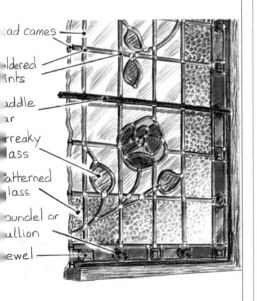

Lead cames

Soldered joints

Saddle bar

Streaky glass

Patterned glass

Roundel or mullion

Jewel

FIG 2.7: *A close up of a leaded light glazed door panel with labels of its key parts.*

Renovating doors with leaded lights

Although you can have leaded light panels removed from doors or windows and professionally renovated, you can make repairs yourself to minor damage. A small crack or gap in a quarry can be covered by applying a false lead strip, while a loose piece of glass can be cemented back with putty. A missing or smashed quarry can be removed by carefully cutting the soldered joints and peeling back the lead *cames*, then having a new piece cut by a local glazing firm (see p59).

Most were coloured all the way through or flashed with a thin coat (which was used for intense colours like red), while some were made with a streaky pattern running through them. Clear or coloured patterned glass, which had a texture applied to one side by metal rollers while it was in its molten state, was usually used. Small roundels, bullions or bullseyes were the scrap centre pieces from the end of the glass makers pipe, which formed when blowing traditional crown glass. In the past they were recycled, but by

FIG 2.8: FANLIGHT OR TRANSOM WINDOW: *With tall ceilings and dark narrow halls, many Edwardian houses still had fanlights fitted above the front door to cast light inside. These were rectangular, either with clear glass featuring the house number or name in the centre, or with coloured glass patterns to complement the door below. During this period, suburban houses further away from city centres were erected on more spacious plots. The hall became wider and the ceilings lower, with a window set to the side of the door rather than above it. This arrangement became the norm by the 1930s.*

Security and Insulation

A new uPVC front door does not suit a period property. White doors are inappropriate and new pre-coloured types rarely match traditional finishes. However, modern doors are good at both preventing drafts and improving security. Although an original timber door may not match u-PVC on these practical points, it is important to take measures to upgrade insulation and locks when renovating an existing or fitting a reclaimed door. Foam or rubber strips stuck around the inside edge of the frame, brush strips at the bottom of the door, a seal or flap across the inside of the letter box and a key hole surround covered by a disc will all help to cut out draughts. Run your hand around the gaps on a windy day to check to see if more measures are required. A proven traditional method for improving insulation is to hang a thick lined curtain from a portiere rod, which will swing out of the way of the opening door. If security is an issue, then make sure the frame is firmly fixed into the wall, with screws every couple of feet as a minimum and three hinges to support the door. An automatic deadlocking rim nightlatch should be fitted, preferably a third of the way down from the top, and a deadlocking mortice lock a third of the way up from the bottom. This prevents the door from being opened from the inside if the glass is smashed. In areas of high crime, you could fit security grills or film across glass and extra locks, although planning permission may be required if you live in a conservation area or a listed property.

the late 19th century, they had become a decorative tool and were inserted into designs, along with jewel shaped pieces, in order to catch the light. In the second half of the 19th century, imitation stained glass with rural scenes, wildlife, historic figures or heraldic symbols painted onto the surface and then kiln fired had been popular, even in modest middle class homes. Although they were rather old fashioned by this time, they could still be used as a centrepiece of a design. Not all designs had colour, some used sheets of etched or sandblasted glass with simple repeating patterns or floral displays within the frosted surface. Another option was to use different textures of clear glass within the leaded lights, although this became far more common in the 1930s.

Door Furniture

The metal fittings on the door were either made from brass with a satin polished finish (rather than the high gloss lacquer on modern pieces), or from cast iron with a black painted surface for the Arts and Crafts inspired property. This latter option had the additional advantage of not requiring frequent polishing, an important consideration at a time when getting servants was becoming a problem. Knobs were almost exclusively used to open the front door, lever handles were not common until after the First World War. Letter boxes or plates could be the decorative centrepiece, with Art Nouveau curvaceous designs distinctive of the period. The size of the flap was usually small, as most mail or parcels would have been received by servants,

FIG 2.10: ESCUTCHEON: *Although small, the cover for the keyhole would still match the style and material of the other metalwork on the door. Teardrop designs or simple metal discs, as pictured here, were two common designs.*

FIG 2.9: BELL PUSH BUTTONS: *The old system of a knob beside the doorframe, connected by cables to bells, was by this time being replaced by modern electric systems and push buttons, as pictured here. The design of the push button to activate it often mirrored the form of the older pull knobs, with a metal disc recessed into the wall, or a wooden or black rosette mounted on top of it with a white button in the centre. The word 'press' was presumably added in case the caller got confused and tried to pull it. Smaller rectangular types became available in the Edwardian period.*

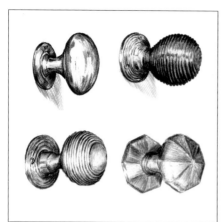

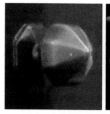

FIG 2.12 (ABOVE): *Door furniture was made from brass (left pair), bronze or black painted cast iron (right pair). Some pieces, like letter plates, could be painted the same colour as the door.*

FIG 2.11: KNOBS: *On many period doors today the knob has been removed when a modern nightlatch was fitted, originally they would have been set lower down at the edge of the lock rail, or in the centre of large or double doors. There was a wide choice of door knob which could be fitted to the front door, although the most common seems to have been a plain round, hexagonal or reeded design, in either brass or black painted iron. The metal disc or rose plate on which they were mounted would often be decorated to match the design on the knob. Arts and Crafts inspired houses could also feature more inventive designs and traditional forms, like the drop ring on Fig 2.15 (see also Fig 4.7 and 4.8 for internal door knobs).*

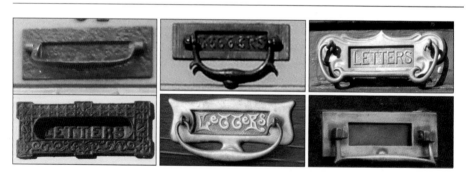

FIG 2.13: LETTER PLATE OR BOX: *Designs could vary from late Victorian types, with a rectangular surround with all manner of geometric profiles and ornate decoration (bottom left), to more stylish Art Nouveau designs with sweeping edges and a plain surface. Some had a door knocker incorporated into the design, others had a fixed bar across the front which acted as a door handle. If there was neither, then a separate door knob and knocker would have been fitted.*

so a modern replica piece with a larger opening may be more suitable when renovating a door. Even little details like the escutcheon which covered the key hole, could feature decoration on the flap which covered it. Mortice locks (set within the door) were common by this period, although older rim locks, which were fitted to the surface of the door and could feature decorative metalwork, were found on some Arts and Crafts houses. A final touch may have been a house number, either set in the glass fanlight above or written on a small oval shaped china or metal plate, which was screwed to the top of the door.

Door Finishes

In the finest homes, the door would be made from a quality hardwood, which was simply varnished or waxed. Oak was particularly desirable, especially for the Arts and Crafts house. In the majority of cases though, an imported softwood was used. This wood was carefully selected from mature trees and will last for centuries if properly cared for, as opposed to the fast-grown types used in mass produced doors today. The Victorian acceptance of fakery was still an influence in this period. Many doors would have originally been grained like the window frames (see Fig 1.16) to make them look like a hardwood. Painting a softwood door in a solid colour was another alternative. Typical colours were a dark green or red, usually with more of a satin finish than the high glosses available today. Although the Queen Anne style inspired the use of white paint, this was only likely to be found on the frame and porch, rather than the door itself. The atmosphere was very sooty and the pavements often muddy, so dark colours or graining were more practical. Some Edwardian houses can be found with a light and dark colour combination used to highlight the door, although this did not become a common finish until after the First World War.

FIG 2.14: KNOCKERS: *These were usually fitted in the centre stile of the door, where there was no knocker built into the letter plate or a separate bell push. They were mostly vertical in form and comprised of a matching pair of discs, or a decorative back plate, with a hollow triangle-shaped or solid piece of various designs hanging from the upper part.*

FIG 2.15: *Arts and Crafts style doors could feature elaborate handmade ironwork, as in this exceptional example from Blackwell, The Arts and Crafts House, Windermere. Sunflowers and the heart were symbols which often featured in their work, with cast iron drop handles also popular. Note also the stylised floral pattern in the band across the centre.*

CHAPTER 3

Exterior Detail

Porches, Balconies, Finials, Rainwater Traps

FIG 3.1: *To complete the exterior of a period house, attention should be paid to the decorative details and functional parts. As with these houses, dating from the 1890s, builders tended to cram the façade with every conceivable feature. Porches, plaques, bands of tiles, bargeboards and decorative rainwater traps all added to create a distinctive and eclectic mix of metal work, ceramics and timber work.*

Although the windows and doors were the focal point of the exterior display Edwardians, like their Victorian predecessors, were rarely happy until every surface had been covered by some degree of decoration or cladding. This could range from mock timber framing, hanging tiles, pebbledash or traditional wall materials revived by Arts and Crafts architects, to terracotta plaques with lavish moulded patterns and stylised symbols, like the popular sunflower. The most distinctive feature of the finer terrace, semi or detached house in this period was the addition of timber porches, balconies and decorative bargeboards, now that restrictions upon the use of wood across the façade had been relaxed. It is these original fittings, fixed by the builder to the structure of the house, and which may either need repair or replacement as part of a restoration project, which are the subject of this chapter.

FIG 3.2: PORCHES: *Timber porches could be unique creations, crafted for an individual property, or more humble structures made from mass produced spindles and decorative parts. They ranged from simple frames bracketed off the wall, to verandas with railings and posts spread across the front or trapped between bay windows. Most today are painted white, as they would have been on houses inspired by the Queen Anne style. However, many were originally painted a colour, varnished or grained to look like a fine wood and would have complemented the doors and window frames.*

FIG 3.3: *Porches which ran as a continuous line across the façade, as in this example above, were a distinctive feature of Edwardian housing.*

FIG 3.4: *Hammered metal hoods (top right), variations of early 18th century types (centre right) and basic bracketed timber porches (bottom right) were often found on Arts and Crafts and Neo Georgian housing.*

FIG 3.5: BALCONIES: *Despite the obsession with privacy, rather unsavoury urban views and the inclement weather, balconies proved a popular addition to the Edwardian house. Some were clearly intended to be used with French doors opening onto a spacious railed area above a porch or bay window, others however seem to have been just a suggestion, with a stretch of timber balustrade in front of a window.*

FIG 3.6: WALL TILES: *Glazed, decorative or plain coloured geometric tiles were often inserted on the walls flanking the front door, or as a plaque on the façade. Some formed simple repeating patterns, with black and white designs becoming popular in the early 1900s. Others had curvaceous and stylised floral patterns influenced by Arts and Crafts and Art Nouveau designers. These colourful insertions are well worth retaining and may give a clue to the colour scheme originally used on the exterior.*

FIG 3.7: TERRACOTTA: *Terracotta plaques and decorative tiles were a distinctive feature of houses in the late 19th century. Some featured the date and name of the property, others were individual tiles set in a row or square. Although there were some inventive designs(as in the jumping frog far left) most were florals with the sunflower (far right), a particular favourite on Queen Anne and Arts and Crafts inspired houses.*

FIG 3.8: TILED PATHS: *One of the most striking features when approaching an Edwardian house are the tiled paths, especially those in fashionable black and white geometric patterns. These intricate mosaics have often been pulled up to install driveways. Where they do survive, they are well worth cleaning (warm soapy water and a scrubbing brush is best, chemical cleaner may damage them) and repairing them where the surface has sagged or cracked.*

FIG 3.9: GATES: *Although metal gates and railings in a variety of historic styles continued to be fitted to houses in this period, wooden gates and railings along the top of brick walls were also popular.*

FIG 3.10: AIRBRICKS AND VENTS: *Even humble air bricks set in the base of the wall and vents positioned in the gable ends of some houses could be decorative in form, or be arranged to form a simple pattern. They are important to keep open and clear of obstructions as they allow air to pass beneath the house or through a loft void to reduce the effects of damp on timber joists. Air bricks close to the ground are particularly prone to getting blocked by soil and plants.*

FIG 3.11: FINIALS: *The ridge of the roof and the end where it meets the gable were often finished with decorative tiles and finials, as in these examples. Although elaborate figures and mystical beasts could still be found on a few houses, most in this period were of a simpler form. The same simplification also applied to ridge tiles. Metal finials and cresting were popular on earlier Gothic houses, but could still be found in the late 19th century. Clay roof tiles with plain ridges became popular during the Edwardian period, to become the standard on most houses after the First World War.*

FIG 3.12: BARGEBOARDS: *The underside of the roof along the top of gable ends was usually finished off with timber bargeboards. Victorian types were often richly carved with large perforations, those in this period however were less elaborate in design, with simple scalloped undersides (top row) or plain boards (bottom row), and often had pendants hanging down from the apex complementing the finial.*

FIG 3.13: RAINWATER TRAPS: *Part of the ethos of Arts and Crafts designers was not to apply unnecessary decoration to their work, but rather to create patterns and beautiful forms out of functional parts. This is evident on the metalwork used on the outsides of their houses, like hinges, handles and most spectacularly on the rainwater traps or hoppers. They could be handcrafted and embellished with floral designs (as in the centre right pair from Blackwell, The Arts and Crafts House). These decorative hoppers were also a feature of Neo Georgian houses.*

Lead Paint

Please note that most paint used on wood and metal surfaces in this period contained lead. If the surface is sound, then just overcoat with another paint. However, if it is flaking and the removal of layers of paint is necessary, then call in a professional decorator. Guidelines on removing lead paint are available online.

CHAPTER 4

Interior Detail

Stairs, Doors, Wall Mouldings, Lighting

FIG 4.1: *With the increased size of many suburban houses in this period, builders had the space and the budget to embellish the interior with fittings like the staircase, wall mouldings and tiled floor in this hallway.*

Stepping inside an Edwardian home, you would have found a much wider range of styles, colours and fittings than on the outside. Speculative builders had to play safe to attract all manner of tenants, and so the style of the façade would rarely be daring. There were far greater opportunities to express the tastes of the occupants inside the home, and with an increasing range of magazines, catalogues and shops specialising in fitting out the interior, families could add their personal touches to each room. This work would have been done by professional builders and decorators, as very few people would have tackled DIY at this date.

Despite the interior reflecting an individual's taste, there were certain rules and fashions which most people adhered too. Within the house there would have been a hierarchy in the order of fixtures and fittings, with the finest saved for the main reception rooms. As you ascended the house to the private bedrooms, the doors, staircase and wall decoration would have become simpler and less expensive. Whereas today we might spend much of our budget on fitted kitchens and bathrooms, in the Edwardian period most money was directed at the drawing room or parlour. This was the most important room and was used to impress guests, or to relax in during the evening. It is also worth remembering that it was only the wealthier families who could afford to furnish a room in a complete scheme. Most people used a combination of hand-me-downs, mixed with the odd new piece when moving in or redecorating. Mixing old and new styles together was accepted so long as there were complementary themes, colours and tones.

Stairs

At the turn of the 20th century, one of the most notable changes in the layout of the home lay just behind the front door. Cheaper land meant that many new suburban houses could be built on a wider plot than before. This extra space enabled some to have a living hall. This was a communal room, based upon a medieval hall and reintroduced by Arts

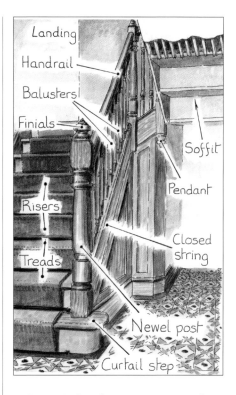

FIG 4.2: *A closed string staircase with labels of its key parts. The handrail and balusters together form the balustrade.*

and Crafts designers, where guests could be received or entertained, with a short flight of stairs rising out of one corner. In narrower houses, the hall had a short length of wooden balusters and a newel post at the bottom. But this was still a significant improvement over the more modest Edwardian homes, where the steps were stuck between walls, either rising from the end of the hall, or between the front and rear rooms.

The main decorative element which you may need to restore or replace is the balustrade. This comprises the newel post and a series of vertical balusters rising up the side of the stairs, which are fixed to the string at the bottom and the handrail along the top. The style of these stairs tends to be a reinterpretation of 17th and 18th century types, with the wooden parts mass produced and available to the builder in various designs, to complement the historic theme of the house. Cast iron had previously been used, but was now unfashionable for staircases. The newel post could be a chunky, turned piece with a finial on top, or squared with carved panels at the sides. The balusters were

FIG 4.4: *A strikingly modern looking staircase designed by C.F.A. Voysey at his own house, completed in 1899. Although the woodwork was painted white, the handrail on the landing upstairs was still unpolished oak.*

FIG 4.3: *A staircase from an Arts and Crafts style house (left) with flat balusters and undecorated newel post inspired by early 17th century types. In more modest houses, a simple arrangement with distinctive slender balusters (right) would have been found. The wood would have usually been stained and varnished, if it was not made from hardwood. Painting it white like some Arts and Crafts houses was rare at this date. A strip of carpet would have been run up the middle, held in place by metal rods. Brass was the traditional material for rods, but black painted versions or wooden strips were also popular as they required less cleaning.*

notably slender in this period, usually less than two inches in thickness, and tended to have a long, unturned lower section and a short upper one. This gave the builder the flexibility to cut them to size on site, so that two or three balusters could sit on a horizontal step, with the turned centre section still rising in a smooth line (see Fig 4.1). Handrails were usually of polished or stained wood, and the rest of the staircase was the same, or painted.

The drive for simplicity and honesty in the Arts and Crafts movement resulted in designs with plain newel posts and balusters in light woods or painted finishes becoming popular in the most fashionable interiors. They were based upon the staircases found in early 17th century farm and manor houses, with simple oak newel posts and plain balusters, or flat planks with a shaped outline (splat balusters). After the First World War, this simple style would become the norm in most suburban housing.

Internal doors

The doors to each room were less flamboyant than those used for the entrance to the house. The standard

FIG 4.6: *Glazed doors were sometimes used between main reception rooms in this period.*

FIG 4.5: *Examples of internal doors. Although oak, mahogany and other fine hardwoods were desirable, most internal doors would have been of a good quality softwood. This was then grained to look like a finer type or painted, sometimes with stencilled patterns on the panels. Stripped pine doors would never have been acceptable!*

Victorian four panelled door was still common, with older style six panel ones fitted in some of the finest houses, to suit the revival in early Georgian architecture. In Arts and Crafts inspired houses, simple plank and batten doors could be used. However, most homes built under this banner were smart, upper middle class homes and still had panelled doors in a fine hardwood, although the arrangement of panels could be inventive and unique. Towards the end of this period, doors with either a large panel for the upper third or a series of full width panels stacked upon each other, became fashionable. Simple versions of this type became the standard form for internal door by the 1930s.

Doors which led into the main reception rooms or faced into the entrance hall would have been the best quality, with fielded panels and the smartest door furniture. As you went upstairs, or into service rooms where guests rarely visited, the panels might be flat rather than moulded. The knobs would also be plainer.

FIG 4.7: *Door knobs were the standard door fitting and could be found in ceramic, glass, brass and other metals. Elaborate examples like those pictured here would be found on receptions rooms, while upstairs they would be plainer. Handles only became fashionable towards the end of the period, with knobs still common in the 1930s.*

FIG 4.8: *Ironwork door fittings from an Arts and Crafts house. These pieces often had a hammered finish, which was both fashionable and didn't require regular polishing.*

FIG 4.9: *Fingerplates were a must on most internal doors. A tall, rectangular plate in brass, copper, tin or ceramic was screwed above the knob, sometimes with a smaller one below. The plates gave an opportunity for elaborate decoration, as in these examples.*

Flooring

Most tenants and owners would cover the floorboards with a range of carpet pieces, rugs or cheaper floor cloths. In the days before vacuum cleaners fitted carpets were rare, floor coverings needed to be removable for easy cleaning. The builder would, however, install a permanent hardwearing or decorative flooring in certain areas of the house. Ceramic tiled floors were a prerequisite for the halls of most middle class houses. They were formed into patterns using geometric shaped pieces in black and white or a range of colours, with a few encaustic decorative tiles in the centre pieces. These were usually surrounded by plain square (called quarry tiles from the French 'carre', meaning square) and rectangular border tiles. Parquet flooring, made from small blocks of hardwood, like oak, were an alternative. Dark red, hardwearing ceramic tiles were usually fitted in service areas.

Wall Mouldings

Strips of wood or plaster with a moulded profile which ran along the wall were more than decorative tools, each had

FIG 4.10: *Black and white ceramic floor tiles were distinctive of the opening decades of the 20th century.*

FIG 4.11: *Examples of a geometric patterned ceramic tiled floor (top) and oak parquet floor (bottom).*

a specific function in the past. Skirting boards protected the base of the wall from knocks and covered up any unsightly gaps between it and the floor. Dado rails, set roughly three foot up, were originally used to protect the wall from chairs pushed up against the side of the room. By the Edwardian period, dados were found mainly in the hall and landing. Picture rails had become fashionable and were a fixing point to hang frames from, often aligned with the top of doors to allow room for a decorative frieze to be fitted above them. Cornices covered up the gaps at the top of the wall, and added a touch of class to a room. Ceiling roses or centre pieces helped to disguise stains from gas lamps and candles suspended below them, some were even perforated so the fumes could be vented outside. However, as electric lights began to be fitted ceiling roses fell from favour.

Arts and Crafts designers tended to not use wall mouldings. They preferred

FIG 4.12: *A common arrangement of wall mouldings in an Edwardian reception room. The cornice at the top had a decorative frieze between it and the picture rail, which ran in line with the top of the door. The skirting below was tall to complement the proportions of the wall above.*

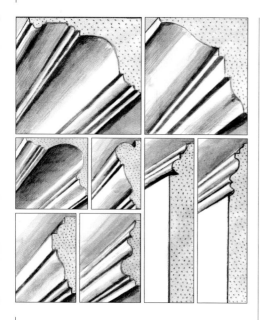

FIG 4.14: *Pictures were hung on chain or wire, then suspended from a metal hook which fitted over the rounded top of the picture rail.*

FIG 4.13: *Examples of cornice (top), picture rail (centre) dado rail (bottom left) and skirting board (bottom right). Those used for hanging or protecting the wall were made of wood. Decorative cornices and ceiling roses were supplied ready made from plaster or papier maché, the latter being cheaper and lighter. The style of the mouldings used on each piece varied to suit the style of the room, however, in general they were less ornate and the depth shallower than those which were used in the mid-Victorian period. Skirting boards, dado rails and sometimes picture rails were grained to look like a hardwood, or painted a dark colour, as this covered up the knocks and scratches that they received.*

either timber wainscot (wall panelling), or a small projecting shelf in place of the picture rail. These light and functional interiors were considered too radical in 1890, but by 1910 had begun to influence the middle class homes. Decorative wall mouldings fell from favour and simpler designs of cornices and plain picture rails and skirtings began to be fitted.

Light fittings

The period from the late 19th century through to the outbreak of the First World War marks a notable change in the way in which houses were lit, as electric lighting became available. The first domestic installation with the new incandescent light bulbs came in 1880. A decade later, electric lighting was still limited to select new housing. However, during the Edwardian period this clean, safe and instantaneous source of power began to be laid on to existing domestic properties. New designs of fittings, shades and light bulbs were produced, although many were still very traditional in style. It was also common for old gas fittings to be converted to electricity. It is worth noting that by 1914, gas lighting was still more widespread, while in rural areas oil lamps and candles were often still the only source of light.

The light fittings installed by builders were in the main adaptations of Classical or flamboyant Georgian style candle sconces (wall brackets), pendants (ceiling lights) and chandeliers (gas versions were known as gasoliers), with extremely busy and ornate brass pipework and embellishments. Art Nouveau designs, endowed with elaborate metal floral decoration, were popular in the early 1900s. Tiffany lamps from America, with their distinctive bronze tree trunk bases and coloured glass shades, could be found in the most avant-garde homes. The Arts and Crafts doctrine of simplicity and functional design seems to have had less of an impact on lighting, although leading designers like W.A.S. Benson produced innovative metal fittings, and medieval and Tudor style candle holders were also used.

It was common for all fittings, including candlesticks, to have shades fitted in the late 19th century. These included globes with etched or cut glass patterns, green and pink glass shades and elaborate silk coolies with tassels and beads hanging around the rim. In the hall, ceiling lanterns with brass frames holding coloured glass were extremely popular. During the Edwardian period, shades lost their frilly trims and became simpler in design, although they might still seem rather fussy to modern eyes.

Bathware

Bathrooms were a relatively new addition to the house at the turn of the 20th century and were mainly found in middle class housing. The working classes still had to bathe in an old tin tub in the living room, while the rich had servants to bring hot

FIG 4:15: *A late Victorian gas pendant light (left) and an Edwardian type (right). Incandescent mantles were introduced in the 1880s, and were small fabric nets covered in a non inflammable substance. They were placed over the flame to create a very bright white hot globe (these mantles needed to be replaced regularly). In 1897, burners were introduced (right) which projected their light down, rather than up towards the ceiling.*

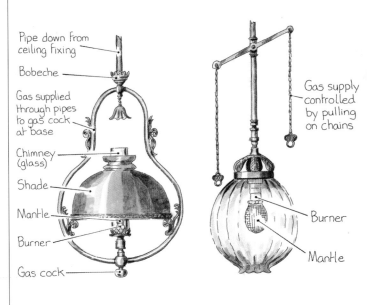

Pipe down from ceiling fixing

Bobeche

Gas supplied through pipes to gas cock at base

Chimney (glass)

Shade

Mantle

Burner

Gas cock

Gas supply controlled by pulling on chains

Burner

Mantle

FIG 4.16: *A brass chandelier, which would have been fitted in a main reception room (top left), a hall lantern (top centre), and a late Victorian wall sconce or bracket light (top right). A Tiffany table lamp (bottom left), a Medieval style ceiling light for a grand dining room or hall (bottom centre), and a copper and brass Arts and Crafts table lamp by W.A.S. Benson (bottom right). Despite the convenience of electricity and the widespread availability of gas, in most homes in this period these fittings would have been complemented by paraffin lamps and candles.*

water up to their private bedroom should they so desire. Enamelled cast iron bath tubs were either boxed in with wooden panelling, or left open on decorative legs. The exterior would be painted in a marble effect or a decorative pattern.

Wash basins (referred to at the time as lavatory basins) were usually glazed earthenware products, with a rectangular shaped top (or angled to fit in a corner) and a variety of round and oval shaped bowls set within. They could be plain white or have a marble effect under the glaze, with the surround and splashbacks often made of real marble. They were

FIG 4.17:
A combination bath and marble topped wash basin in their original wooden panelling with brass fittings.

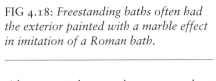

FIG 4.18: *Freestanding baths often had the exterior painted with a marble effect in imitation of a Roman bath.*

FIG 4.19: *Brass taps with capstan handles were widely used in this period.*

either mounted on a mahogany or walnut stand with a cupboard, or mounted on decorative cast iron brackets and open beneath.

The water closet, as the toilet was still referred to at the time, was usually in a separate room and not part of the bathroom. The basin could be supplied white, or with floral patterns decorating the exterior and sometime interior

FIG 4.20:
An Edwardian water closet with wooden seat.

surfaces of the enamelled earthenware basin. The seat was made from mahogany, walnut or oak, often with a squared off rear and conventional hinges. The cistern was nearly always mounted high up, and the brass chain or rod hanging down ended in a ceramic or wooden handle. Not everyone had access to mains water and sewage, so earth closets in which an amount of soil or cinders was dropped down the pan when flushed, were still common.

Kitchen

Forget the modern fitted kitchen, the best an Edwardian family could have expected when they moved into a new house would have been a sink on a base unit, a range cooker and a built in cupboard. The other parts, like dressers and tables, would have been freestanding furniture. Sinks would usually be an earthenware Belfast or butler type with a wooden drainer. Any cupboards would be plain painted, with wooden or metal knobs.

FIG 4.21: *A detail from a large Edwardian kitchen with a built in cupboard and drawers.*

CHAPTER 5

Fireplaces

Surrounds,
Grates, Tiles

FIG 5.1: *Edwardian fireplaces ranged from compact cast iron pieces to imposing features incorporating cupboards and even seating. They reflected the fashion for displaying ornaments, with shelves fitted within the surround, or as part of the overmantel above it, as in this grand example.*

There is one feature which was the centrepiece of each room and has such importance and variety that it justifies a chapter of its own, the fireplace. The fireplace was also the only source of heat in the days before central heating.

FIG 5.2: *A fireplace with labels of the key features. The stone, timber or cast iron surround was usually referred to at the time as the mantelpiece or chimneypiece. The sides (jambs) and top (lintel or frieze) supported the mantel shelf, which in this period was deep to accommodate ornaments. The stone, brick or tiled hearth was important to ensure any coals or sparks from the fire did not ignite or damage the flooring. Overmantels were separate pieces fitted above the mantel shelf and were a distinctive feature in middle class housing during this period, usually with a central mirror and shelves and cupboards to the sides. The grate in which the coals were held was fitted within the opening and were usually made as a single piece, with angled sides for ceramic tiles and a canopy above it.*

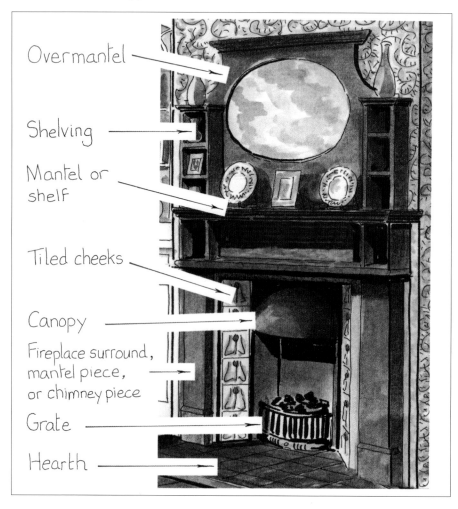

Overmantel

Shelving

Mantel or shelf

Tiled cheeks

Canopy

Fireplace surround, mantel piece, or chimney piece

Grate

Hearth

Fireplaces

The fireplace comprised of a surround, chimney piece or mantel piece, with a cast iron grate set within it. A tiled hearth in front of the fireplace protected the floor from sparks and coal dust. In smaller houses and bedrooms, the surround and grate could often be supplied as one cast iron piece. It was also fashionable to have an overmantel positioned above the surround. This could incorporate a mirror, shelving or glass fronted cupboards, or a combination of all these features.

In Arts and Crafts homes, the overmantel often spread out on either side, so that the fireplace formed a small central part of a large bookcase or display cupboard. Another favourite of this style was the reintroduction of inglenooks, as found in old farmhouses. A brick or stone fireplace could be set within the wall, with intimate seating placed on either side.

FIG 5.3: BLACKWELL, THE ARTS AND CRAFTS HOUSE, WINDERMERE: *This is possibly the finest Arts and Crafts house currently open to the public. Designed by M.H.Baillie Scott, his interiors epitomise the key ideals and innovative design championed by the movement. He had a masterly control of space and light and used local materials to create rooms which were both grand and intimate (see Fig 0.3). This inglenook fireplace set within an arched recess in a corner of the dining room features a traditional wood burning grate (which Arts and Crafts designers preferred to coal) and blue and white Delft tiles. This idea of creating an intimate space with seating was copied in more modest houses built in this style with some featuring small windows, as here, to illuminate it with natural light.*

FIG 5.4: *Charles Rennie Mackintosh was Britain's leading exponent of Art Nouveau and an inspiration to many designers on the Continent. His stylised floral decoration, as featured here, was distinctive but too avant-garde for most tastes at the time, and this otherwise plain fireplace is more typical of the 1930s.*

FIG 5.5: A cast iron register grate and surround with distinctive Art Nouveau style floral decoration. Although today these pieces are usually supplied in black or a polished metal finish, most would have originally been painted either in one or two colours, or with an effect to imitate wood or stone. The angled cheeks would have originally held bold patterned ceramic tiles.

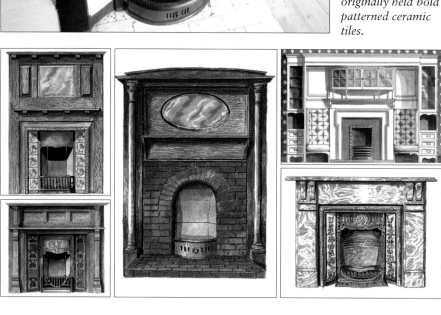

FIG 5.6: Examples of Edwardian fireplace surrounds, some with overmantels featuring shelves, cupboards and mirrors. The central example was a style which remained popular after the First World War.

FIG 5.7: FIREPLACE MATERIALS: *Marble was still desirable in this period (top right). It is prone to staining, but can be cleaned through a process of careful washing and brushing with soapy distilled water, and using marble cleaner or a poultice to remove ingrained dirt. Slate was a cheaper alternative and was usually painted or enamelled to look like marble or another stone finish (top left). Oak and walnut were popular woods used in this period and could feature inlaid patterns (bottom left). Arts and Crafts fireplace materials were either left in their natural finish, or painted to match the furniture in a room (bottom right). Wood and metal surrounds were usually supplied whole while marble and slate came in sections.*

FIG 5.8: REGISTER GRATES: *The central cast iron piece which held the coals and could feature a canopy and tiled cheeks is referred to as the grate. From the mid 19th century, they had a hinged plate called a register covering the opening to the flue to control the draw (see Fig 5.9). A cast iron grate can be cleaned up by removing rust with a wire brush and painting with a black stove paint, and then polishing the whole piece with graphite grate polish. Brass parts can be cleaned with polish and steel with a thin oil.*

Installing fireplaces

Original fireplaces should be retained at all costs. They add value to the property and are an attractive feature in a room. They can also be accommodated in a modern decorative scheme (the fixings were usually plastered over so it can be disruptive and expensive to remove them).

Unfortunately, many fireplaces have long since been ripped out when central heating was installed, or in more recent times because of their value. Therefore, you will often have to install a reclaimed or replica surround and grate as part of a restoration project. It is important to ensure that the floor and wall where it is sighted are sound. The fireplace is surprisingly heavy and trimmer arches or extra timber were originally fitted below the hearth to help support it. If you are planning to light the fire, then you must have the chimney cleaned and inspected. Make sure that the stack, pot and flaunching (the cement which beds it into the top of the chimney) are sound. You can also have a liner fitted within the flue. A liner improves the performance of the fire and seals it to prevent gases escaping into other rooms. If you are making significant changes, then you will need to comply with building regulations. Chimney engineers can be found by contacting the National Association of Chimney Engineers: www.nace.me.uk. While the National Association of Chimney Sweeps has a list of registered sweeps in your area: www.nacs.org.uk. Air needs to be supplied from below, with a good draw above, for the fire to burn properly. As houses are more insulated now, the former can be a problem. An additional vent may need to be installed in the floorboards in front of the hearth, or to one side to give sufficient air flow, but not a draught across the room. It is also important that the dimensions of the flue and the fireplace opening are in the proportions of around 1:7-1:10, if it is larger than this then fitting a baffle or canopy across the top of the grate may help. If the fire is not going to be used, and you intend to block the flue up, then make sure a vent grill is fitted in the fireplace and a cap or similar arrangement put on the top of the chimney pot, so that air can still be drawn up through the stack to prevent damp.

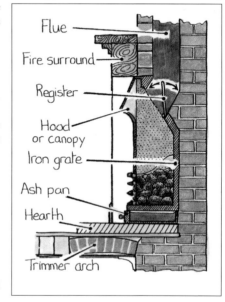

FIG 5.9: *A section through a register grate with labels of the key features.*

Labels: Flue, Fire surround, Register, Hood or canopy, Iron grate, Ash pan, Hearth, Trimmer arch

FIG 5.10: CANOPIES OR HOODS: *These were a distinctive addition to register grates in the late 19th and early 20th centuries. Most were cast iron (centre), with patterns to complement the style of the piece. In the most fashionable interiors, brass or copper with a hammered finish or a decorative design (top and bottom) could be found.*

FIG 5.11: TILED PANELS: *The tiles up the sides of the grate were available as a set. They either formed a single pattern, as in this colourful example, or as a series of repeated designs.*

FIG 5.12: *Examples of tiles fitted into fireplace grates. Those in the late Victorian period tended still to use busy floral designs, with browns and greens prominent (top half). Edwardian tiles could be found with lighter colour schemes and stylised Art Nouveau designs (bottom half). These tiles were held in place by frames on the rear of the grate. To remove or change them it is best to pull the surround out to access them. As this can be tricky, it is possible to replace a damaged tile by inserting a replacement one which has been cut down slightly so it can be worked into the grooves on either side.*

Coal scoop

Coal box

Fender

Fire screen

FIG 5:13: *There were a number of accessories which could be found around the hearth, in addition to the set of tools used for maintaining the fire itself. Decorative fire screens were positioned to protect people from excessive heat, coal scoops and boxes were used to store the fuel, and fenders were sometimes fitted to the edge of the hearth. Some simple grates without canopies might still have had a fabric smoke deflector (see Fig 5.8 top right), although by this date these were usually just for decoration.*

FIG 5.14: *A small detail which tells you much about life in a house in this period, is a bell push or pull next to the fireplace. It was used to summon servants to the room and emphasises the fact that the family spent much time talking, reading and socializing around the fireplace.*

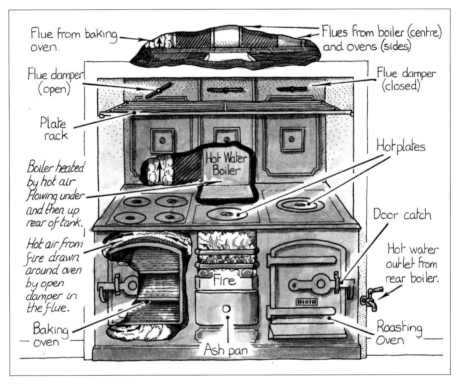

Flue from baking oven.

Flues from boiler (centre) and ovens (sides)

Flue damper (open)

Flue damper (closed)

Plate rack

Boiler heated by hot air flowing under and then up rear of tank.

Hot air from fire drawn around oven by open damper in the flue.

Baking oven

Hot Water Boiler

Hot plates

Door catch

Hot water outlet from rear boiler.

Fire

Roasting Oven

Ash pan

FIG 5.15: *Range cookers were still a standard fitting in the kitchen, scullery or rear living room of most houses in this period. In general, they were cast iron appliances with a combination of oven and boiler positioned around a central enclosed fire, and hot plates on the top surface. They were notoriously hard to control by unskilled hands, and required constant maintenance and regular cleaning. They fell from favour after the First World War, when reliable gas or electric cookers and freestanding boilers became widely available. Today, modern variants like Agas (introduced in the late 1920s) and range style gas and electric cookers are more appropriate for the kitchen of a period property, however in some rural properties an original one may still be found and be worth retaining for its decorative value.*

Care, Repair and Renovation

Renovating a House

It can be disheartening to hear poor advice given to house buyers, or see destruction carried out on some period homes, as original fixtures and fittings are ripped out in an attempt to upgrade or renovate the property. Instead of upgrading the original front door with new security locks and a coat of paint, an expensive new door might be fitted. It is easy to get carried away and completely gut a room, rather than keep original parts and integrate them into a new scheme. An Edwardian fireplace can be painted and new tiles fitted to make it blend into the background, so it is retained as an asset for when you sell the house.

A good example of the problem is with double glazed windows, as a whole generation of home owners have been inundated with adverts and advice. It is now believed that new uPVC windows will always add value to a property. This is usually true of most post-war houses, where the timber used was generally not designed to last more than a few decades. Modern houses also suit large sheets of silky smooth glass. However, it has the opposite effect on an Edwardian house, where the sash windows should last for centuries with a little care and attention. In this instance, it is well maintained and draft free original fittings which can add value to these period properties. Replacement double glazing usually only lasts 20 to 30 years before it needs to be ripped out again. The glass mists, handles break or materials deteriorate and then become unfashionable. A good example of the problem is aluminium framed windows from the 1980s, now they can reduce the value of a property as they look so out of place. In time, glossy white uPVC might also become outdated, as new coloured window frames become available.

The issue in the past with windows and other fittings, was that it was so much easier to call up a double glazing company to come and fit new, replacement windows which would reduce the drafts and noise and not require painting. However, the internet and various companies that have sprung up to help you renovate your period home have changed this situation. Today, you just need to go online to find lists of companies that will renovate your windows, fit them with insulation strips, put in noise reducing secondary glazing and paint them so that they do not need maintenance for another decade or two. Fortunately, the web has also opened up access to reclamation yards and antique shops dealing in period house fixtures and fittings, so if you need to replace parts it is just a quick click on your mouse to find long lists of suitable parts.

The following websites are a good starting point to finding original parts for your house:

www.salvo.co.uk
www.buildingconservation.com

www.periodproperty.co.uk
www.arcsal.com
www.theheritagedirectory.co.uk

These are some examples of the types of sites which offer a good range of original or replica parts:

www.wardantiquefireplaces.co.uk
www.reclamation-yard.co.uk
www.regency-antiques.co.uk
www.antiquedoorfittings.co.uk/
www.mongersofhingham.co.uk
www.theperiodironmonger.co.uk
www.stoneagearchitectural.com
www.snobsknobs.co.uk
www.arcreclamation.com
www.britainsheritage.co.uk
www.finest-stair-parts.com

Before you commence any work on your Edwardian home, it is important to establish if your house is listed or within a conservation area. If it is the former, then you will need consent for any changes outside, and probably inside as well. If it is the latter, then the limitations tend to be just with the parts of the house which are visible from the street. It is a good first step to consult with your local conservation officer before spending any money on plans and fittings, or ask neighbours with similar properties for their experiences and details of any local builders they can recommend.

If you plan to do most of the work yourself, then there are a number of guides which have been published specifically for period properties.

I would recommend:
Period House: How to repair, restore and care for your home, published by Collins and produced with English Heritage. It is an invaluable source of information, even for just occasional maintenance jobs.

There are also a range of books by Haynes covering maintenance of period houses which are worth looking out for.

I have also written the following books which include more general information on Edwardian houses.
The Edwardian House Explained covers all aspects of building, from the structure down to interior details.
Arts and Crafts House Styles describes this influential movement, the style of the houses and types of furnishings and decoration which were popular at the time.

For more information and to buy these and my other books, please visit:
www.trevoryorke.co.uk and **www.countrysidebooks.co.uk**

For general information about houses from this period, the following website is an excellent source of information:
www.bricksandbrass.co.uk

There are also a number of magazines covering period houses which list suppliers and services for old properties. The Listed Property Owners Club and their magazine *Listed Heritage* are an excellent example of these:
www.lpoc.co.uk

Please note that the author and publisher take no responsibility for the quality of service provided by any of the companies listed.

Glossary

Acanthus	A leafy plant which was a popular Classical decorative form.
Anaglypta	An embossed patterned wallpaper from the Greek word meaning 'raised ornament'.
Anthemion	A honeysuckle leaf and flower design.
Architrave	The moulded wooden or stone surround of a door or window.
Ashlar	Large blocks of stone cut square with fine joints.
Balusters	Individual turned supports for a balustrade (supporting the rail up the side of stairs)
Bargeboard	External vertical boards which protect the ends of the sloping roof on a gable and were often decorated.
Bay window	A window projecting from the facade of a house of varying height but always resting on the ground.
Bow window	A bay window with a curved profile.
Cames	Lead work which holds the small panes (quarries) of glass in a window.
Carytides	Human half figures.
Casement window	A window which is hinged along the one side.
Cast iron	A brittle metal formed in moulds, whereas wrought iron is pliable and forged into decorative patterns.
Chinoiserie	A French term for Chinese design and influence.
Classical order	A style of Classical architecture which is most easily recognised by the style of the capital used on the columns.
Concave	Inward curving surface.
Convex	Outward curving surface.
Cornice	A decorative moulding which runs around the top of an external or internal wall.
Dado	The lower section of a wall. The moulding along the top of this is the dado rail.
Dormer window	A window projecting out of the roof with a flat or gabled top.
Eaves	The section of the roof timbers under the tiles or slates where they meet the wall, usually protected by a facia board.
Egg and dart	A decorative moulding with egg shapes divided up by the pointed end of a dart.

Façade	The main vertical face of the house.
Faux	A French word for 'imitation'.
Fielded panel	A panel with a raised central section with chamfered or angled sides.
Flue	The duct for smoke from the fireplace up into the chimney.
Fluted	A column or pilaster with concave narrow grooves running vertically up it.
Fretwork	A geometric grid of interlacing lines formed into a band or panel.
Frieze	A large horizontal ornamental border along the top of a room or panelling.
Gable	The pointed upper section of wall at the end of a pitched roof. A Dutch gable is shaped with concave and convex curves.
Glazing bars	The wooden or metal divisions within a sash which hold the panes of glass.
Herringbone	A pattern formed from short angled pieces which appear like a horizontal zigzag. Used in brickwork, masonry and parquet flooring.
Inglenook	A recessed space for a fire with seating to the sides.
Jambs	The sides of an opening for a door or window.
Joists	Timber, concrete or steel beams which support the floor.
Laminated wood/ Plywood	A board made from thin sheets of wood bonded together with the grain in opposite directions to make a strong and stable material used in furniture.
Linoleum	A flooring made from linseed oil, cork dust, wood flour and other ingredients set on a canvas backing (often called Lino).
Lintel	A flat beam which is fitted above a door or window to take the load of the wall above.
Lyncrusta	A deeply embossed wallpaper
Marquetry	Patterns in the surface of furniture made from different coloured inlaid wood.
Moulding	An ornamental strip of wood or plaster with a decorative profile formed from concave, convex and angled elements.
Mullion	The vertical member dividing up a window. A low, long window with only mullions is known as a mullion window.
Muntins	The vertical members in a frame, for instance in a panelled door. Sometimes used to refer to a glazing bar or mullion.
Newel post	The end post of a balustrade on a staircase, often with a decorative finial on top.
Oriel window	A projecting window on an upper storey.

Palmette	A stylised palm leaf motif.
Panelling	Wooden lining of interior walls with vertical muntins and horizontal rails framing the panels.
Parquet floors	A geometric floor design formed from pieces of inlaid wood, often in short rectangles laid out in a herringbone pattern.
Pebbledash	An external render with small stones or pebbles thrown at the final coat. It was originally left in its natural state, although it is often seen painted today.
Pilaster	A flat column.
Render	A protective covering for a wall made from two or three layers of cement.
Reveal	The sides (jambs) of a recessed window or door opening.
Roughcast	A render with small stones mixed within to give a rough texture when dried. The finish was finer than pebbledash and was usually finished with coats of whitewash.
Sash window	A window with two sashes (a frame with glazing) which slide up and down on counterbalanced cords.
Scroll	An ornamental motif based on the end of a rolled up piece of paper or scroll.
Size	An adhesive based mixture of varying thickness which is used to seal plaster walls and can form decoration.
String	The side support panel for a staircase.
String course	A horizontal band running across a façade and usually projecting.
Swag	An ornamental piece of fabric or garlands draped between two points.
Terracotta	Fine clay moulded and fired into decorative pieces, usually left unglazed on Arts and Crafts buildings.
Tracery	The stone ribs forming geometric shapes and intersecting patterns in the upper half of a medieval window.
Transom	A stone or wooden horizontal member dividing up a large window.
Turned	A rounded block of wood carved by rotating it, while cutting a profile into it with a tool.
Vernacular	Buildings made from local materials in styles and with methods of construction which have been passed down within a distinct area.

A message from Trevor Yorke: I hope you have enjoyed this book. If you have, and want to learn about others I've written, then please go to my publisher's website **www.countrysidebooks.co.uk**

My titles are available in all platforms – as softcover books and as eBooks.

Follow me on Facebook at trevoryorke-author, and click 'Like' to keep up to date with new titles and offers.

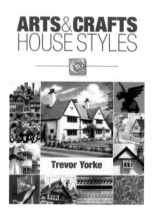

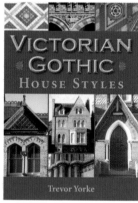

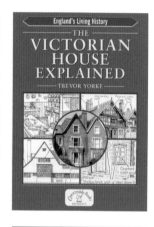

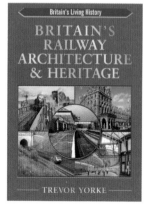

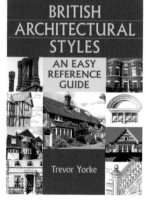

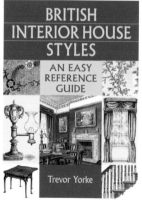